❧❧

DAVID AND GOLIATH

Contributing Writer
Marlene Targ Brill

Consultant
David M. Howard, Jr., Ph.D.

Illustrations
Thomas Gianni

Publications International, Ltd.

A long time ago in the town of Bethlehem, there lived a boy named David. He and his brothers were sons of Jesse. David was very special to God, and God watched over him.

David was a shepherd. Every day when David went to tend the sheep, he brought his harp with him. He would play the harp to calm the sheep and to make the day go by faster.

Nearby in Bethlehem lived Saul, the king of Israel. Saul was an unhappy man. At one time he had loved and respected God. But then one day Saul displeased God. After that, Saul became very sad.

A servant suggested that they find someone to play the harp for Saul. He thought some music might cheer him up. Another servant knew that David played the harp. So David went to the palace to play for the king.

David's music did make King Saul feel better. He asked Jesse to let David stay at the palace.

Meanwhile, David's brothers joined Saul's army. Once when David was visiting home, Jesse said, "I hear the Philistines are ready to fight. I am worried about your older brothers. Take this food to them. Then come back and let me know how they are."

David awoke early the next day, picked up the sack of food, and started on the trip.

7

As David neared the army camp, he heard yelling. The two armies were lined up and ready to fight.

"Today I dare the army of Israel," roared a giant Philistine soldier named Goliath. He was trying to make one of Saul's men fight him. "Give me a man to fight. If he wins, we will be your servants. If I win, you will be our servants."

Saul's soldiers were afraid. This man was so big and strong. But David shouted, "I will fight the giant Goliath myself!"

David's brothers told him to be quiet and go home, but David would not listen. King Saul heard about David's promise. "You are just a boy who tends sheep," he said. "Goliath has been a warrior since he was a child."

"I know I am a shepherd boy," David answered. Then he told the king how he had rescued sheep from bears and lions. "God has saved me from wild animals," David told Saul. "God will save me now."

༈༈

King Saul knew what had to be done. "Go and may God be with you!" the king said. Saul wanted to help David, so he gave him heavy armor. But David was not used to it. The armor was too heavy for him.

David removed the armor. Walking to a nearby stream, he picked out five smooth stones. He put them in his pouch, grabbed his sling and his shepherd's crook, and started off to fight the giant.

Goliath marched toward David. The sunshine glared off the shiny helmet on the giant's head. In Goliath's hand was a fierce-looking spear that weighed more than fifteen pounds!

The giant looked down at David. He thought the boy was too young and small to fight. Was someone playing a joke on him?

"Am I a dog that you come to me with sticks?" yelled the angry Philistine. "Come here and I will feed you to the birds and wild animals."

David answered Goliath, "You come at me with a sword and spear. But I come in the name of God who protects the army of Israel. Today I will strike you down. Everyone will know that there is a God in Israel. And that God does not save by spear and sword."

The angry Philistine ran at David. David pulled a stone from his bag. He fixed it in his sling and flung it toward Goliath with all his might.

The stone struck the giant on the forehead. Goliath fell to the ground. David grabbed the giant's sword and held it high to show both armies he had won. The Philistines ran away with Saul's army right behind them.

When Saul heard about David's victory, he was so happy! He knew that God was with David.

After that, David lived in the palace like a royal son. Later he became king and ruled Israel for many years.

ጉየ